SandCastle

Keeping the Peace

Being a Peacekeeper

Pam Scheunemann

Consulting Editor, Diane Craig, M.A./Reading Specialist

ABDO
Publishing Company

Published by ABDO Publishing Company, 4940 Viking Drive, Edina, Minnesota 55435.

Printed in the United States.

Credits
Edited by: Pam Price
Curriculum Coordinator: Nancy Tuminelly
Cover and Interior Design and Production: Mighty Media
Photo Credits: BananaStock Ltd., Comstock, Eyewire Images, ImageState, Stockbyte

Library of Congress Cataloging-in-Publication Data

Scheunemann, Pam, 1955-
    Being a peacekeeper / Pam Scheunemann.
       p. cm. -- (Keeping the peace)
    Includes index.
    Summary: Describes everyday actions, such as being polite, following rules, and being fair, that can help to keep the peace.
    ISBN 1-59197-558-1
    1. Conduct of life--Juvenile literature. 2. Peace--Juvenile literature. [1. Peace.
2. Conduct of life.] I. Title.

BJ1631.S265 2004
170'.44--dc22
                                                                          2003057783

SandCastle™ books are created by a professional team of educators, reading specialists, and content developers around five essential components that include phonemic awareness, phonics, vocabulary, text comprehension, and fluency. All books are written, reviewed, and leveled for guided reading, early intervention reading, and Accelerated Reader® programs and designed for use in shared, guided, and independent reading and writing activities to support a balanced approach to literacy instruction.

Let Us Know

After reading the book, SandCastle would like you to tell us your stories about reading. What is your favorite page? Was there something hard that you needed help with? Share the ups and downs of learning to read. We want to hear from you! To get posted on the ABDO Publishing Company Web site, send us e-mail at:

sandcastle@abdopub.com

SandCastle Level: Transitional

A person who
is thoughtful of
others keeps the
peace.

Jan and Kay like to keep the peace.

Jan is making the symbol for peace with her fingers.

Doing what parents ask is a way of keeping the peace.

Joe washes the car without complaining.

Being polite is a way of keeping the peace.

Debbie's friends clap for her after the show.

Being quiet is a way of keeping the peace.

Morris is quiet in the library.

Following the rules helps keep the peace.

Rich, Pam, Lola, and Chris talk about the rules before they play tennis.

Keeping a secret can keep the peace.

Fay puts her trust in Nancy when she shares a secret.

Keeping your promise is a way of keeping the peace.

Ellen promised she would feed her hamster, Ralph, every day.

Being fair is a way of keeping the peace.

Katie and Mark take turns choosing which video game to play.

Having fun together is a way of keeping the peace.

Rob and Nora are having fun baking bread.

What can you do to keep the peace?

Glossary

polite. having good manners or showing consideration for others

promise. to give your word that you will do something

rule. an established regulation that tells you what you should and should not do

symbol. an object that represents something else

trust. reliance on the character, ability, or strength of a person or thing

About SandCastle™

A professional team of educators, reading specialists, and content developers created the SandCastle™ series to support young readers as they develop reading skills and strategies and increase their general knowledge. The SandCastle™ series has four levels that correspond to early literacy development in young children. The levels are provided to help teachers and parents select the appropriate books for young readers.

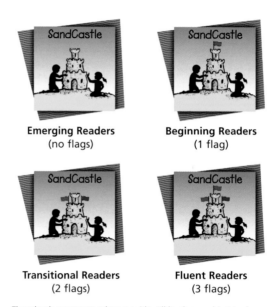

Emerging Readers
(no flags)

Beginning Readers
(1 flag)

Transitional Readers
(2 flags)

Fluent Readers
(3 flags)

These levels are meant only as a guide. All levels are subject to change.

To see a complete list of SandCastle™ books and other nonfiction titles from ABDO Publishing Company, visit **www.abdopub.com** or contact us at:

4940 Viking Drive, Edina, Minnesota 55435 • 1-800-800-1312 • fax: 1-952-831-1632